London

Published by
Colour Library International Ltd.
80/82 Coombe Road
New Malden
Surrey UK.
Tel. 01 942 7781

Printed by
Creaciones Especializadas de Artes Gráficas, S. A.
Barcelona - Spain
D. L. B.-1498/75

ISBN 0 904681 03 3

London

A picture-book to remember her by

Published by Colour Library International in Association with the British Tourist Authority

Introduction

Although the pictures in this book cover nearly two thousand years of history, from London's crumbling Roman Wall to its spectacular new Post Office Tower, they have been classified, for your convenience, by *subject* rather than by *period*.

So, if your interest lies in famous landmarks, in such irresistible magnets as Big Ben and Buckingham Palace, St. Paul's Cathedral, Westminster Abbey and the Tower of London, you will find them grouped conveniently together in the first of its pages. Or, if your weakness is for *people*, such as the London policeman, the city man in his bowler or the guardsman in his busby, for theatre and music, for shops and market places, or for lively, colourful pubs, category by category you will discover them in other sections of this book.

London has something for everyone — for the lover of pageantry, history, art treasures, parks, squares, roads or rivers. And, whatever your preferences may be, wherever you roamed or whoever you met in this most exciting of cities, this book will call them back to mind.

Contents

Page 3. The Houses of Parliament by night, viewed across the River Thames from County Hall. When Parliament is sitting a light will be seen shining at the top of the clocktower.

Facing page, Queen Boadicea's statue, with Big Ben — clocktower of the Houses of Parliament — in the background. Queen Boadicea defeated the Roman invaders of Britain in AD 59.

Famous landmarks

Buckingham Palace — official London residence of Her Majesty the Queen. Acquired by George III in 1762 and re-modelled by John Nash, who began his work in 1834. The Palace provides a noble setting for that most striking and spectacular of daily events Changing the Guard.

The old and the new — the red-brick gate-tower of St. James's Palace, built by Henry VIII in 1532, with a 20th century office block on Millbank towering far behind it. Not only did Henry VIII live in the Palace of St. James but so did his successors Edward VI, Mary, the Great Queen Elizabeth I and the Hanovarian monarchs until 1837. Ambassadors to Britain are still accredited to "Our Court of St. James's" although, since Victorian times, St. James's Palace has been used only for levees, courts and other ceremonies.

Westminster Abbey where, since 1066, all but two of England's kings and queens have been crowned and where many of them lie buried. Also in the Abbey is Poets' Corner where memorials to such famous bards as Chaucer, Shakespeare and Milton will be found.

The Chapel of Henry VII, right, in Westminster Abbey which dates from 1502 — a masterpiece of architectural grace and beauty. Hanging above the stalls of the Chapel and the tomb of Henry VII and his queen are the resplendant banners of the Knights of the Bath.

The Coronation Chair upon which, in Westminster Abbey, every English monarch has been crowned since Edward I. Encased in the Chair is the Stone of Scone, traditional seat for the crowning of Scotland's kings, which was brought to London by Edward I in 1296.

Perhaps the most famous of all London landmarks – the Houses of Parliament, or, as they are still sometimes called, the Palace of Westminster. Before them flows the Thames, spanned by Westminster Bridge and behind and beyond them are Westminster Abbey, Westminster Cathedral and the towers and spires of Pimlico. Parliament, first summoned in 1265, met until 1834 in the Chapel of St. Stephen which was destroyed by fire. The first stone of today's Houses of Parliament was laid in 1840 and the building was completed in 1857.

Now welded snugly into the Houses of Parliament is Westminster Hall, left, one of London's most historic buildings. With its massive hammer-beam roof Westminster Hall housed, for centuries, the principal law courts of England. Here were sentenced such ill-starred men as Sir Thomas More and Charles I.

The House of Lords, meeting place of the noblemen who form the "upper house" of Britain's Parliament. Their proceedings are presided over by the Lord High Chancellor whose seat, the Woolsack, stands before the Throne which is occupied only when the Queen opens Parliament.

Yeoman Warders, above, known
popularly as Beefeaters, guard
Traitor's Gate at the Tower of London.
Much of the Tower stands little
altered since it was built in 1078. It
houses, among other treasures, the
Crown Jewels and a magnificent
collection of armour of all periods.

The collection of armour and
weapons displayed in the Armoury
at the Tower of London was founded
by King Henry VIII. It includes the
tilting armour worn by this substan-
tial monarch, together with suits of
steel "tailored" for other (and slim-
mer) kings of England.

The Tower of London, from the south bank of the River Thames. Its great central keep — the White Tower — was built by William the Con-queror, of stone from Caen in Normandy. It was in this White Tower that Sir Walter Raleigh and Guy Fawkes were imprisoned. Near the water's edge may be seen the low and gloomy archway of Traitor's Gate through which such notable State prisoners as Queen Anne Boleyn, Lady Jane Grey, Sir Thomas More and the Duke of Monmouth passed unhappily into the Tower.

The Tower of London seen from Tower Bridge. Built originally as a fortress the Tower has served also as a palace and as a prison. Its Norman keep is surrounded by two walls, one of which, dating from the 13th century, has thirteen towers.

14

The River Thames, above, from dockland, fringed by wharfs and warehouses and with ships loading and unloading. Spanning the river, with St. Paul's Cathedral in the distance behind it, is Tower Bridge, which ranks high among London's famous landmarks. The first of London's bridges encountered when approach is from the sea, Tower Bridge, right, is a triumph of Victorian engineering. Each of its two drawbridges weighs 1,000 tons and can be raised in 1$\frac{1}{2}$ minutes. It dates from 1894 and its distinctive silhouette has become one of the city's trademarks.

Piccadilly — the heart of London and once the hub of the Empire. With its glittering lights it is especially impressive by night. Poised above its centre island is the renowned statue of Eros — one of the first statues ever to be cast in aluminium.

St. Paul's Cathedral, left, from Waterloo Bridge with the Victoria Embankment to the left and Blackfriars Bridge to the right. Moored by the Embankment are the Discovery and the Wellington, the latter a one-time Admiralty sloop now the Livery Hall of the Honourable Company of Master Mariners.

Trafalgar Square, above, famous alike for its column erected to perpetuate the memory of England's great sailor, Nelson, for its fountains and for its pigeons. Among the buildings, which encircle Trafalgar Square are the National Gallery, and St. Martin's-in-the-Fields — the parish church of Buckingham Palace.

New landmarks

The Post Office Tower, right, London's highest landmark – 620 feet from ground level to masthead. With three observation platforms, from which superb views of London may be enjoyed, a cocktail lounge and a revolving restaurant, the Post Office Tower has quickly become popular with visitors to London.

One of the first of London's new landmarks – built immediately after World War II – is the Royal Festival Hall, left, on the south bank of the Thames. This modern concert hall now has as neighbours the Queen Elizabeth Hall; the Purcell Room and the Hayward Gallery.

Curving upwards among the tree tops of Holland Park is the arresting roof of the exhibition hall of London's Commonwealth Institute, left. Dating only from 1962 this impressive structure provides a centre for the presentation of Commonwealth countries and of their artistic and industrial achievements.

Pageantry and Ceremonial

Whether encountered at home in the Tower of London, or elsewhere on ceremonial occasions, London's Yeomen Warders or Beefeaters, are unforgettable. They are shown above, on Tower Green, beating the bounds in uniforms which have remained unchanged since Tudor times.

One of the most photographed elements of London pageantry, are the troopers of the Household Cavalry, top, who stand sentry daily at Horse Guards. Red tunics and white plumes distinguish Life Guards ; blue tunics and red plumes, Royal Horse Guards.

London's year-round programme of ceremonies is highlighted by such royal occasions as the Opening of Parliament and Trooping the Colour. Pictured, right, is Her Majesty the Queen, colonel-in-chief of the Household Brigade, taking a salute at Buckingham Palace.

Trooping the Colour, below, which takes place early in June, each year, in honour of the Queen's birthday, is London's most spectacular military pageant. This many-splendoured event is staged on the great parade ground behind Horse Guards. Her Majesty rides side-saddle from Buckingham Palace to Horse Guards at the head of the Household Cavalry. There she inspects the regimental colour which is trooped and reviews the Guards as they march and countermarch, to and fro across the parade ground.

The Lord Mayor's Show, a colourful procession believed to date from the 13th century. It occurs annually, in early November, when the newly-elected Lord Mayor — surrounded by pikemen and riding in a gilded coach — proceeds in State through the City.

With their tunics of scarlet and gold and their fabulous bearskin busbies, the foot-guards of the Household Brigade, who stand guard before London's royal palaces, are a feature of London life with which the visitor falls in love at first sight. Pictured, left, is a sentry of the Household Brigade on duty at Clarence House, London home of the Queen-Mother, which adjoins St. James's Palace — another royal establishment at which foot-guards are to be seen at close quarters.

The Old Guard of the Life Guards, white plume, red tunic, is shown, right, returning from duty at Horse Guards where there has been a mounted guard every day since 1751. On State occasions it is the function of the Household Cavalry, of which the Life Guards are a part, to protect the person of the Sovereign. Their daily parade, to and from the Horse Guards, adds colour and animation to London's streets and is one of the city's principal attractions.

London's river — the Thames — is shown here sweeping away beyond the Houses of Parliament. Behind Big Ben — the tower with the clock — are, first, Westminster Bridge, then Charing Cross Bridge and, behind that, Waterloo Bridge. Cruising the Thames by river-launch is one of the most enjoyable ways of seeing London. Whether you travel upstream to Richmond and Hampton Court or downstream to the Tower of London or Greenwich, you'll find that the Thames flows past a wealth of interesting places.

London's River

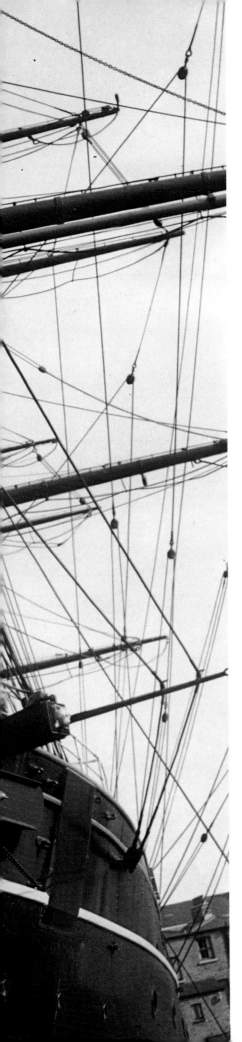

Down river from London is Greenwich, famous for its meridian, its palatial Royal Naval College, top, and its National Maritime Museum, partly located in historic Queen's House. And, en route to Greenwich, are such waterfront hostelries as The Angel, at Rotherhithe, above.

Preserved permanently in dry dock at Greenwich lies the Cutty Sark, left, last and most famous of the old tea-clippers. Housed on board is a colourful and evocative collection of ship's figureheads which vividly recall the romantic days of sail.

Queen Elizabeth Hall, above, part of the contemporary concert hall/art gallery complex which stands on the south bank of London's river. This new concert hall has as its neighbours the Royal Festival Hall, the Purcell Room and the Hayward Gallery.

Lambeth Palace, centre, for seven hundred years the London home of the Archbishop of Canterbury. Its chapel, dating from 1245, suffered serious damage during the war; but still surviving are its Lollards' Tower of 1431 and its red-brick Gothic gatehouse of 1490.

St. Paul's Cathedral, right top, seen from Wren's View on the south bank of the River Thames. Sir Christopher Wren, who designed this great cathedral and supervised its construction, is said to have chosen this stretch of London's waterfront as a vantage-point from which to watch his masterpiece take shape.

Along the north bank of the Thames beside Waterloo Bridge – and occupying the site of a palace – runs the long facade of Somerset House, right, below. Once the home of the Royal Academy, Somerset House now shelters a group of Government departments.

One of London's most delightful
vistas is to be found in St. James's
Square, right. Here, framed by trees
and green lawns and with the pil-
lared portico of the Haymarket
Theatre as a backdrop, prances a
statue of King William III.

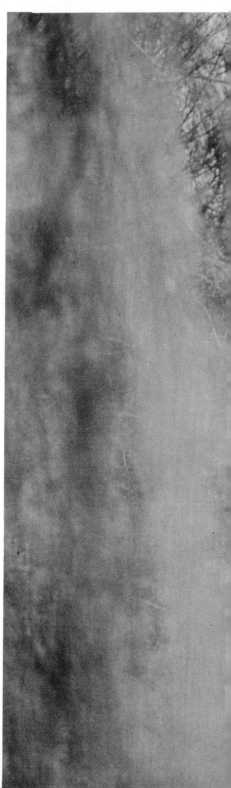

Music in the open air may still be enjoyed during summertime in many of
London's parks and pleasure gardens.
In Hyde Park, beneath the trees —
and only a stones throw from the
waters of the Serpentine —
performances at the Bandstand,
above, are an ever-popular attraction.

Perhaps the most beautiful of
London's parks, St. James's, right,
owes its origin to King Henry VIII
who, finding it a marsh, transformed
it into a deer park! Pictured, from
the bridge which spans its lake, are
the domes of Whitehall.

Parks and Squares

On the northern fringe of Hyde Park, with Marble Arch nearby, a space is reserved where orators — and their audiences — may air their views. This is Speakers' Corner, above, where messages political, social and religious are delivered to a critical world.

Soaring above the tree-tops of Embankment Gardens — where workers from nearby offices lunch and listen to concerts is Cleopatra's Needle, above. This famous obelisk, which reached London with difficulty from Heliopolis in 1878, has a counterpart in Central Park, New York.

34

Grosvenor Square, left, in the heart of Mayfair, traces its associations with America back to 1785 when John Adams, the first American minister to Britain, set up house there at No. 9. Today the square is the home of the United States Embassy.

There can be few more agreeable (and rewarding) ways of spending a warm summer's evening in London than by watching Shakespeare performed at the Open Air Theatre in Regent's Park, left. The theatre is pleasantly located in Queen Mary's Rose Garden.

Side by side with Hyde Park lie Kensington Gardens, above, a pleasure ground famous for its royal palace (now the London Museum), its Peter Pan statue, its Albert Memorial, its Round Pond — and for the fountains and Long Water pictured above!

London's Treasures

Few cities are as rich in art treasures as London. And nowhere in London (or indeed the world) will you find so magnificent and unforgettable a collection of European paintings as that which is housed in the National Gallery, left.

The National Portrait Gallery, below, abounding in pictures and bronzes of men and women famous in British history and drawn or sculpted, for the most part, by their contemporaries. Here, arranged chronologically, are portraits of kings and queens, statesmen, artists, scientists.

London' newest and oldest are encountered side by side at the Guildhall Museum, above, in the City. For here, in a series of recently completed exhibition galleries, are exhibited fragments, unearthed by the excavators, of bygone London cities – Roman, Saxon, medieval.

Trafalgar Square above, is one of London's best known landmarks, laid out by Sir Charles Barry in 1829. From the top of the 182 ft. high column the statue of Nelson looks down on the Square, the fountains and its famous pigeons. Among the buildings which encircle Trafalgar Square are the National Gallery and St. Martin's-in-the-Fields, which is the parish church of Buckingham Palace.

The company of Sotheby's below, is the worlds oldest and largest auctioneers of fine art pictures, wines, jewellery, silver, furniture, books, works of art, glass, musical instruments, and antiquities. Visitors can attend auctions and see a fabulous range of works, normally on view before the auction.

Founded in 1753 — a public lottery was set on foot to raise the money — the British Museum, left, is today an establishment of mammoth size. In it is stored a wealth of material of historic and artistic interest *plus* the National Library.

One of the world's most important museums — the Victoria and Albert, right, with its fabulous collections of ceramics, oriental art, costumes, furniture, theatre art, musical instruments, jewellery, metalwork, glass, textiles, tapestries, pictures, sculpture and books. Covering an area of twelve acres, the Victoria and Albert is a treasure house of fine and applied art. Its treasures include seven great Raphael cartoons, an unrivalled collection of works by Constable, the national collections of miniatures and watercolours — and the Great Bed of Ware.

Sir John Soane's Museum, left, the Soane Museum, was once the private house of this famous architect. Soane died in 1837 but, in this most fascinating of museums, his spirit still presides over an extraordinary collection of antiquities, paintings, drawings, books, and furniture together with the tomb of Sarah Siddons' dog Fanny! Among the pictures are two series by Hogarth (the Rake's Progress and The Election), several Canalettos and works by Reynolds, Turner, Lawrence and Watteau.

The Geffrye Museum, left, in London's Shoreditch, is located in a group of tree-shaded 18th century buildings which were once the almshouses of the Ironmongers' Company and which date from 1715. The museum contains a fascinating collection of furniture, domestic articles, woodwork and fixtures rescued largely from demolished houses. These exhibits are displayed in a series of 'period' rooms which show how middle class homes in Britain were furnished and equipped from Elizabethan times to the present day.

The Wellington Museum, above, at
Apsley House is, like London's Soane
Museum, an establishment which
must be visited. The House — an in-
trinsic part of the museum — was
once the home of the Duke of
Wellington who defeated Napoleon
at Waterloo. Together with important collections of Spanish, Italian
and Dutch paintings (which include
works by Valasquez, Murillo,
Corregio, Pieter de Hooch and Jan
Steen) Apsley House contains many
relics of the great Duke — medals,
decorations, swords, flags, porcelain, silver plate ; and snuff-boxes.

The Wallace Collection, famous for its many 17th century paintings by Watteau, Boucher and Fragonard and for its French furniture and Sèvres porcelain. Included among the treasures of the Wallace Collection is the Frans Hals portrait of "The Laughing Cavalier", left.

London's famous Tate Gallery, above, the world's largest picture gallery was founded initially to accommodate the main national collection of British paintings. Today it includes among its exhibits, an impressive array of works by modern artists of many countries. Notable

among its paintings by British artists are works by Turner and Blake ; and among works by 19th and 20th century artists paintings by Cézanne, Bonnard and Braque and sculpture by Rodin and Epstein.

A city for all seasons

In whatever season of the year you explore London you will find her in good countenance. In springtime gay with flowers ; her parks and window boxes bright with snowdrops and crocuses . . . and with daffodils 'that come before the swallow dares and take the winds of March for beauty'. For Londoners love flowers and flowers love London — as our pictures show. Left — a Chelsea window box ; and bottom left, just one small corner of Hyde Park with Park Lane beyond.

In summertime it is, perhaps, the *greenery* of London which most impresses and delights the visitor — wide expanses of green lawn and surprising stretches of woodlands. Typical of such woodlands are those surrounding the lakeside concert-shell in the grounds of Kenwood House, below. Here open-air concerts may be enjoyed. Kenwood, a stately mansion upon the heights of Hampstead, houses an important collection of pictures — largely English 18th century.

While autumn in London is no longer a season of mists and mellow fruitfulness it still has very much its own atmosphere. The days grow shorter and, through the golden half-light, the horse-riders trot along famous Rotten Row, left. But, crowning London's year is winter — when the night falls early and the friendly lights of London glitter along every street and in every square. Pictured in Trafalgar Square, is the Christmas tree which Norway presents to the city every year.

"John Keats lived here" — and it was in the garden of this house, near the hill top at Hampstead in north London, that the poet wrote his Ode to a Nightingale. The house is now a Keats Memorial and Museum.

On the Thames Embankment in Chelsea, just beyond Battersea Bridge, stands the house in which the novelist Mrs. Gaskell was born. That was in 1810 when Chelsea, now very much a part of London, was still little more than a country village.

Literary London

Perhaps the best-known literary shrine in the English-speaking world is Poets' Corner, right, in the south transept of Westminster Abbey. Here you will find not only memorials to many celebrated writers but the graves of Chaucer, Browning, Tennyson and others.

Cheyne Walk, Chelsea. left, famous for its literary and artistic associations. It was here that George Eliot lived and died in 1880, a neighbour of Dante Gabriel Rossetti. And in Cheyne Row (a 'tributary' of the Walk) Thomas Carlyle and his wife had their London home.

Much frequented by Dr. Johnson, whose portrait hangs above his favourite seat, and by Oliver Goldsmith —the Cheshire Cheese, a 17th century tavern in Wine Office Court off Fleet Street. It is still the haunt of men of letters.

London is the background against which a host of famous fictional characters played their parts. None of these is better known than Sherlock Holmes whose many strange adventures put Baker Street, and the gas-lit world around it, securely on the map.

London for children

With its pageantry, its historic buildings, its museums and art galleries,
its river launches and its Zoo,
London is a wonderland for children. Outstandingly popular is the
Science Museum, above, with its
vintage locomotives and aeroplanes
and its wealth of working models.

Irresistible, too, is the London
Museum, left, in Kensington Palace.
Included in its collection — and
fascinating to the young — are treasures illustrating the history of
London . . . flint implements . . . fire
engines . . . toys from the 16th century onwards . . . and a model show-
ing the Great Fire.

The Bethnal Green Museum, far left,
a branch of the Victoria and Albert
Museum, has its childrens' section,
renowned for dolls and dolls' houses
of yesteryear and for the furnishings
and accessories with which such
dolls' houses were equipped.

London Zoological Gardens,
"The Zoo", in Regents Park, contains
many thousands of animals
and birds and is a favourite haunt of
children. Of special interest to young
visitors are the elephants, camels,
giraffes, chimpanzees, lions, tigers—
and the giant panda.

The Zoological Society of London

Among the friendliest birds in the world—and the boldest— are the pigeons which strut and flutter among the spectacular fountains of Trafalgar Square. Feeding these insatiable birds (and being photographed whilst doing so) is an experience which every child enjoys.

The statue of Peter Pan, the boy-who-never-grew-up, which has long made Kensington Gardens a place of pilgrimage for London's children. Stroking the ears of the rabbit, at the base of this famous statue, is now an old established childhood custom.

Children love butterflies. And in the Natural History Museum there are a quarter of a million of them. Together, of course, with such spectacular displays as those to be seen in the Whale Gallery and in the room marked Dinosaurs.

And, whether they are marching on foot to Buckingham Palace or trotting on horseback to Horse Guards, the colourful members of the Household Brigade are an unfailing and unforgettable attraction both to the young and to the young at heart.

At Madame Tussaud's Waxwork Exhibition, below, in addition to its models of the famous and the infamous are the London Planetarium designed and equipped to educate the young and a thunderous representation of the Battle of Trafalgar devised to entertain them.

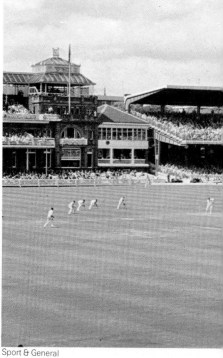

Syndication International

Sporting London

A highlight of London's sporting year is the Boat Race, above, rowed every spring, by crews from the universities of Oxford and Cambridge, along 4¼ miles of the river Thames. Notable, too, is the Head of the River Race in which 100 boats take part.

Derby Day, top, far left, when that most famous of all horse-races, the Derby, is run, is perhaps the greatest event in the whole of London's sporting calendar. Occurring early in the summer, the Derby takes place on Epsom Downs, only 16 miles from London. It attracts racing enthusiasts of every social strata—from costermongers to crowned heads!

With almost a dozen professional football clubs, London is surely the football centre of the world. And it is football which has made Wembley Stadium where Britain's Cup Final, left, is played each year—one of the most famous sports arenas.

Wimbledon, below, far left, perhaps the best-known place in the world of tennis, is a suburb of south London. At midsummer each year the All England Lawn Tennis and Croquet Club stages there, that most celebrated of all tennis occasions, the Wimbledon Fortnight, when the Open Championship of the World is won.

Cricket, that most English of all games, may be enjoyed at its leisurely best at either of London's two great cricket grounds—Lords, pictured centre, or the Oval—where Test Matches are played, against teams from the ends of the earth.

London's villages

Villages galore have been engulfed by growing London. Yet many of them retain much of their individuality. Typical of such die-hard villages is Strand-on-the-Green, left, standing on the bank of the Thames between Chiswick and Brentford.

Dulwich, above, a south London village, is famous for its college, founded by the Shakespearian actor Edward Alleyn who died in 1626; and for its Picture Gallery, designed by Sir John Soane and housing a fascinating collection of pictures.

Shepherd Market, right, in the very heart of London, has managed to survive for 200 years or more. Built on land belonging to a Mr. Shepherd, it occupies the site of a market, the May Fair, abolished by George I.

Other London villages famous for their enduring charm and for the famous men who were associated with them are Highgate bottom left, Blackheath top left and Hampstead, above. On Highgate Hill Dick Whittington, 'thrice Lord Mayor of London', heard Bow Bells and retraced his steps. At Blackheath Wat Tyler and Jack Cade rallied their rebel hosts—and James I introduced golf to the south. While at Hampstead lived and worked such celebrities as Keats and Constable. Romney, du Maurier and Galsworthy.

The Café Royal, left, was part of Regent Street even in the days of Nash's famous quadrant and was patronised by such celebrated artists as Sickert, Orpen and Augustus John. Much of its original Edwardian splendour has been retained.

Pubs and restaurants

Today, London's facilities for good eating and good drinking are unrivalled. Her friendly pubs – like the Grenadier in Belgravia, pictured left, which abound in every corner of the town, are also splendid places in which to *meet* the British.

The Cheshire Cheese, right, has one of London's most famous restaurants. A 17th-century inn, once frequented by Doctor Johnson whose portrait hangs above his favourite seat, it is still, to this day, the haunt of men of letters and learning.

Many a London restaurant can trace
its history back into the past – to
Edwardian, Victorian, Georgian days
and earlier. Among these is
Hatchetts', pictured above, founded,
as Hatchetts' Coffee House, in 1702 ;
an establishment which figured
in the drawings of Hogarth and was
patronized by Beau Brummell.

In recent years a host of new restaurants have sprung up in London.
Several of these, like Flanagans in
Baker Street which is pictured right,
have modelled themselves on restaurants of the past . . . on establishments of the days of Sherlock
Holmes and Mr. Pickwick.

In the Elizabethan Rooms, above, in
Kensington where candle-lit
Elizabethan feasts are staged nightly
— with pretty 'serving wenches' in
attendance to fill your cups with
mead and claret — and with the music
of the lute accompanying the
singing of Elizabethan madrigals.

London's people

Part of the pomp and circumstance of the Lord Mayor's Show, which is staged annually in London, are the plumed and helmeted Pikemen.

Uniformed doormen are a feature of many London establishments. The doorman at the Royal Lancaster Hotel has a special magnificence.

Fashions change, but in London the mini skirt may well have come to stay. Indoors and out, wherever he goes, the visitor will find it.

A sign of the times in swinging London is its crowds of longhaired, picturesquely-clad teenagers. Chelsea's King's Road is a favourite haunt.

Every year a new Lord Mayor of London is carried to the Law Courts in a golden coach driven by this resplendent Coachman.

Yet another often-encountered Londoner is the Ticket Collector on the fabulous system of railway lines which criss-cross the metropolis.

Buttoned and be-feathered "Pearlies" are still to be found haunting London's East End pubs or parading its streets on holiday occasions.

There's no better way of seeing London than from the top of a bus. Meet there, too, the friendly "Clippie" who sells you your ticket.

Carving the roast beef of old England in many a London restaurant and crowned by his tall white hat is the genial and imposing chef.

Pacing to and fro, in any of those sheltered backwaters the Inns of Court, London's lawyers are to be seen in their wigs and gowns.

The Yeoman Warder, or Beefeater, with his colourful Tudor uniform, is a much photographed feature of the Tower of London.

A gold-mine of useful information, and the very personification of London, is the helpful, helmeted policeman or "bobby".

On many colourful occasions the trumpeters of the Household Cavalry are to be seen, mounted on their light grey horses.

That familiar London figure the Chelsea Pensioner is an inmate of the Chelsea Hospital, founded by Charles II for old soldiers.

London is a city for flower-lovers. Violets, daffodils, white heather . . . you can buy them all, in season, on London's streets.

Winter visitors to London may well have seen — and heard — chestnut sellers offering their wares. Roasted chestnuts are a London speciality.

Show Girls may nowadays be seen the world over. But London, with its host of theatres and night spots, certainly has its share of them.

The pavement artist may still be seen adorning London's paving stones with pictures and placing his upturned cap hopefully beside them.

Visitors to London who arrive by train will often find that the Porter at the railway station is the very first Londoner to greet them.

It pays to advertise and one of London's oldest means of doing so are the Sandwich Men who tramp the gutters of her crowded streets.

Buskers, or street musicians, have long been a colourful feature of London life. Pictured are members of The Happy Wanderers group.

Sports results or the latest political crisis — the newspaper seller on his busy street corner keeps London in tune with the rest of the world.

The Lord Mayor's City

At the very hub of the City of London stand the Bank of England and the Royal Exchange. The former, to the left in our picture, is sometimes referred to as the Old Lady of Threadneedle Street. The Royal Exchange was founded, originally, in the days of Queen Elizabeth I.

St. Paul's Cathedral which dominates the City of London was designed by Sir Christopher Wren and built – between 1675 and 1710 – to replace its predecessor, Old Saint Paul's, destroyed by the Great Fire of London in 1666. Wren lies buried in the Cathedral and above his tomb, in Latin, is inscribed the phrase ; "Reader, if thou seekest his monument look around."

The Church of St. Mary-le-Bow, top, renowned for the famous Bow Bells which are housed in its tower. St. Mary-le-Bow church was restored and re-dedicated in 1964. In 1966 the King of Norway unveiled there the Norwegian Resistance Memorial.

Among the modern buildings which now border the street known as London Wall, large sections of London's Roman Wall may still be seen. These date from the first century A.D. A further section of the Roman Wall survives in America Square near the Minories.

Lombard Street, which is reputedly, the richest thoroughfare on earth! Soaring above Lombard Street is the Church of St. Edmund King, famous for its buttressed steeple and one of the thirty or more City churches built after the Great Fire by Sir Christopher Wren.

The Monument in King William Street (named after William IV) was built by Wren to commemorate the Great Fire of 1666. A hollow, Doric Column, 202 feet high, the Monument has a caged gallery near its top. This may be reached by a rewarding climb of 311 steps!

Famous for its open-air market
which is held on Sunday mornings is,
left, London's Petticoat Lane, now
named Middlesex Street. Perhaps
the most famous thoroughfare in the
East End of London, Petticoat Lane
lies off the Whitechapel Road only a
stone's throw from Liverpool Street
Station. For cockney spirit Petticoat
Lane has no equal.

Portobello Road, right, just north of
Notting Hill Gate — has been des-
cribed as London's most rewarding
street market. Whilst many of its
traders are indeed experts in their
own fields of the antique — pictures,
jewellery, silverware, cut glass and
the like — bargains *are* to be found
there. At its best and busiest on
Saturday mornings.

London's street markets

Bustling with crowds every moment of the day and every day of the year London's Oxford Street, pictured below, can rightly be regarded as one of the finest shopping centres in the world. In its great department stores almost everything can be found.

In London's Chelsea, for generations the home of the artist and his model, shoppers find the King's Road, mid centre, a fabulous place for all that is newest and gayest in fashion. And King's Road, too, has its art galleries and antique stores.

In recent years, with swinging London making a name for itself in the world, Carnaby Street, bottom centre, has become a name to conjure with. For shoppers who are young in years or spirit . . . eager to keep up with the times ; or ahead of them.

Burlington Arcade, left, which caters for those who buy only the best, runs parallel to Bond Street — from Piccadilly to Burlington Gardens. It is famous for its beadles who not only add to its colour but keep it free from stray dogs !

While Piccadilly Circus, below, has important shops of its own it is famous, also, as a focal-point from which great shopping streets radiate. Notable among these are Regent Street and Piccadilly — both superb for clothing, silverware and books.

Famous shopping streets

London theatres have chequered careers. The "Old Vic", above, started life in 1818, as the Royal Coburg where music hall perform- ances were staged. Today, it is the London home of Shakespeare. The Coliseum, right, long famous for its musical shows, is now the head- quarters of the Sadler's Wells Ballet and Opera. But the Royal Court Theatre, below, where Shaw, Galsworthy, Granville Barker and others were often presented to the world, today, true to tradition, houses the venturesome English Stage Company.

Theatres

Famous both for its ballet and its opera is the Royal Opera House, in London's Bow Street – the opera house known the world over as Covent Garden. Pictured ... is a scene on stage, above, and in the celebrated Crush Bar, Inset.

The Theatre Royal, Haymarket, was built in 1820. It is associated with such famous names as Charles Keen, Edwin Booth, Ellen Terry and Beerbohm Tree whose mammoth productions at Her Majesty's Theatre – just across the road – are a part of stage history.

A wigged attendant at Drury Lane Theatre, right. "The Lane" occupies a site where theatres have stood since 1664. In the first of these, destroyed by fire in 1672, Nell Gwynne made her first appearance as an actress and, possibly, as an orange girl!

Hampton Court, the Thameside palace which Cardinal Wolsey presented – perhaps a little reluctantly – to King Henry VIII, is located midway between Westminster and Windsor. The palace boasts three ghosts – those of Henry's wives Catherine Howard and Jane Seymour ; and of Sibell Penn who was nurse to his son Edward. Hampton Court is famous for its Maze, its astronomical clock and its Christopher Wren Orangery. Its handsome state apartments house a magnificent collection of furniture and of pictures by such painters as Kneller and Lely.

Geoffrey Hart

Around London

Hatfield House, right, twenty miles north of London, home of the Marquess of Salisbury and one of the finest country houses in England. In its West Gardens stands the old Royal Palace where Queen Elizabeth I was imprisoned as a princess.

Stoke Poges Church, left, in the shadow of which the poet Gray wrote his famous Elegy and where he lies buried. Stoke Poges, less than twenty miles from London, is only two miles from the sylvan splendour of Burnham Beeches.

Deep in the woodlands of the Kentish Weald (and less than thirty miles from London) lies Ightham Mote, left, one of the finest moated manor houses surviving in all England. Begun in 1340 – during the reign of King Edward III – Ightham Mote was further developed in early Tudor times and completed during the reigns of Queen Elizabeth I and King James I. Its impressive 14th century Great Hall – with its original oak-timbered ceiling still intact – is one of the most impressive in existence.

Polesden Lacey, right, an elegant Regency villa standing on high ground, twenty miles south of London, among the woodlands of Surrey. Designed by Robert Cubitt, the house contains the Greville Collection of tapestries, furniture and paintings by Lely, Lawrence and others.

Windsor Castle, below ,which lies beside the Thames some twenty miles west of London. Initially a hunting lodge it has been the country home of English sovereigns for nine hundred years. Its state apartments are a treasure house of pictures, by Rembrandt, Van Dyck, Rubens and others.

Kew Gardens, right, officially known as the Royal Botanical Gardens, were founded in 1759 by Princess Augusta the mother of King George III. A feature of the gardens is the Chinese Pagoda which towers above the trees and glass-houses.

Osterley Park, in Isleworth to the west of London, a great house which dates from 1577 but was re-built in 1761 by Robert Adam.

Richmond, Surrey — most delightful of near London riverside towns — boasts splendid views, a celebrated park and the gateway of a palace.

Syon House, across the river from Kew Gardens, historic home of the Duke of Northumberland. The estate has an extensive Gardening Centre.

The Cathedral, above, at the ancient city of St. Albans in Hertfordshire, twenty miles to the north of London. St. Albans claims to possess the oldest inhabited house in England — a tavern called The Fighting Cocks.

Waltham Abbey, right, beside the river Lea, was founded by Harold, the last of England's Saxon kings. It was here that Harold knelt to pray before setting out to fight the fateful Battle of Hastings.

Chartwell Manor, far right, top, in Kent, "the garden of England". For many years the home of Sir Winston Churchill and still rich in paintings — by him and of him — and in such relics as uniforms and trophies.

The cathedral and rooftops of Canterbury far right, below, seem to reflect the timeless legends of the Black Prince's exploits, the tragedy of Thomas á Becket and the Roman occupation of Durovernum. By way of contrast, part of industrial history is also preserved here in the form of the charming engine "Invicta", one of the earliest locomotives.

Index

Index